Things
that *Flow*

Things *that* *Flow*

Humor, Poetry, and Essays about Rivers and Life

K. S. LUBINSKI

Things that Flow
Humor, Poetry, and Essays about Rivers and Life

iUniverse books may be ordered through booksellers or by contacting:

*iUniverse
1663 Liberty Drive
Bloomington, IN 47403
www.iuniverse.com
1-800-Authors (1-800-288-4677)*

ISBN: 978-1-4917-8865-3 (sc)
ISBN: 978-1-4917-8864-6 (e)

Library of Congress Control Number: 2016904778

Print information available on the last page.

iUniverse rev. date: 4/07/2016

To anyone who has worked on a river and said, "It's not about me, my job, agency, or program. It's about the river," thank you for your efforts and inspiration. As the world continues to demand more and more from its natural resources, dedication like yours is the only thing that will save it.

To my wife, Sara J., thanks for sharing the path with me.

To my son and daughter, Ben and Sara E., this stuff, as you know, is what I think and care about. The values I'd like to pass along are in here, although some may be hidden under the surface, like the mussels we couldn't see and had to find with our fingers and toes.

Contents

Preface

Being drafted into the infantry, completing airborne training, and serving in Vietnam taught me two lessons: The first was to enjoy life to the fullest, especially by avoiding boredom, mediocrity, and people who do not want to learn. The second was to try to make a difference, somehow, somewhere.

I had been interested in science and conservation since spending as many days as possible in my youth fishing with my father. So when I got out of the service, I committed to getting an advanced education in sciences that support natural resource management. Luckily, I found a path that led to river ecology, and I was able to rub shoulders with people who knew how rivers worked.

Book learning used up too many years, but as a result, I was able to get two jobs that allowed me to experience the Illinois and Mississippi Rivers up close. With colleagues, I collected fish from all kinds of river habitats. I dived through eighteen inches of ice on the main channel of the Mississippi one January searching for dormant catfish and mussels at the edges of dredged material disposal sites. Over time, I was fortunate to visit and work with now lifelong friends on other large rivers around the world. These experiences helped me and others inject credible science into several emerging river-management programs.

Along the path, rivers became the basis and joy of my adult life. That first lesson mentioned above has paid off, although I still owe the Illinois and Mississippi Rivers a thing or two.

I've published my share of scientific papers, but I've also realized the limitations of science when it comes to reminding others how much we humans depend on—*need*—nature. It's a message that is told best through stories and poems. An important but now forgotten nineteenth-century scientist once said, "Science is always necessary, but never sufficient." Bingo.

I haven't succeeded, to my satisfaction, at making a difference. The rivers of my life seem unchanged in response to my scientific efforts. Fortunately, all by themselves, rivers give birth to stories at every bend and sandbar, and it is by conveying such stories that I hope to encourage greater river awareness and appreciation. This book is my attempt at becoming a whisperer about rivers. Including items about life and work seemed perfectly natural, because life, work, and the river have unerringly flowed together for me. If some of these ditties make you smile or tear up, please let me know. If they make you see a river that is already or is destined to become *your* river, don't waste time telling me. Tell someone who wants to get or stay elected.

Acknowledgments

Sara J. Lubinski, landscape artist extraordinaire, provided the images for "The River is …" and "Spring Break."

Nancy North, friend and lover of stories, provided timely and vital shots of encouragement.

Introduction

I take a lot of comfort from my relationship with the river. It has helped me find a level of internal peace that was missing in my younger years. From what I've read, I'm not alone in this regard. Rivers clearly affect a lot of people in positive ways. Still, many others never get the opportunity to step into a jon boat, explore a side channel, watch mayflies emerge, or dig their toes into cool mud on a hot summer day. Most of the pieces in this book are intended to help these folks experience some of what happens when river science is your calling.

My father taught me, without words, that work is more than a way of making money. A good job is one that is both challenging and rewarding, one that makes you tired, pumps you up when you've done a task well, makes you happy to wake up, and makes you look forward to the next day. When you have such a job, it and life become codependent, flowing together. That is one reason I included pieces about life and work in this collection. I haven't just had good jobs; I've had good jobs associated with great rivers, and the rivers' presence seems to underlie all of my life's experiences and relationships.

Many of the pieces here are more about the relationships between work, life, and the river, as opposed to focusing on only one of these subjects. Relationships are complex, and I know that complexity is attractive to some but frustrating to others. Also, as much as we prefer control, uncertainty is as common on the river as it is in life. You rarely know what is around the next bend. As a result, I've avoided putting the pieces that follow into any predictable order. While the pieces are loosely linked, they act independently, another organizational characteristic of rivers.

Several of these pieces are presented as the thoughts of a character, Miss Sophia, who is introduced in the author's note at the beginning of "A Preference." I started writing the first of these journal items as an experiment and immediately enjoyed the freedom of letting someone else tell the story. Miss Sophia has river smarts and a different way of expressing what she sees and feels. I learn from her.

In his book *A Story of Six Rivers: History, Culture, and Ecology*,[1] Peter Coates suggests that rivers "are good to think with." He describes Marcus Aurelius sitting on the banks of the Danube while making war with the Germanic tribes, considering the universe as "one living thing." The pieces that follow came about because the Mississippi River has been good for me to think (and smile) with. I invite you to find a place along your river and ponder any images, trivial or monumental, that come to mind. They will appear. The river will see to it.

Filthy Rich

Let's go down to the river and see what we can see.
You can be your own self there; I think that I'll be me.
We can talk to strangers there as if they were old friends.
Or we can simply ponder life; I guess it all depends.
Although they call him "Old Man," I want to be that free.
Let's go down to the river and see what we can see.

Let's go down to the river and do what must be done,
even if it's nothing more than lying in the sun.
We can watch the cuties and let them see us too.
Maybe we can tell them lies and swear that they are true.
If the fish bite, we can spend the whole day having fun.
Let's go down to the river and do what must be done.

Let's go down to the river and get us filthy rich.
We won't need to gamble, just take off every stitch.
Float above the sand and mud, squeeze it with our toes,
let his water wash it off, though why God only knows.
Golden castles can't be built unless we scratch the itch.
Let's go down to the river and get us filthy rich.

That Old Man, he won't mind, if we share his soul.
He might even join right in. That might be his goal.

Let's go down to the river and let him teach us how,
to shuck off all our city fears, appreciate the now.
Freedom must be savored, for how long does life last?
Till death the river teaches; "Steer the future, keep the past."
If life is like a jon boat trip, let's ride up on the bow.
Let's go down to the river and let him teach us how.

Taming the People

In 2010, a friend and expert hydrologist invited me to present some thoughts about the health of the Upper Mississippi River at a conference in Kolkata, India. I like to travel and had never been in that part of the world, so I quickly accepted. I was unexpectedly treated to one of most memorable presentations I've ever seen.

A hydrologist from the Indian Statistical Institute, Professor Sengupta, at least eighty-five years old and weighing no more than a hundred pounds, had to be helped onto the stage by a graduate student. Wearing a necklace of orange and yellow flowers that had been presented to him as a man deserving of the highest respect, he finished his speech about the Ganges River with a simple but formidable admonition to the engineers in the room. He filled his lungs, pointed directly at the engineers (most of whom had spent their entire careers designing flood control structures), and said, "Don't tame the river. Tame the people!" This from a man whose densely populated and generally poor country has suffered from countless great floods.

How rare it is to hear something so important and profound expressed in so few words. Of course hydrologists and engineers, no matter where they live, have no inalienable right or authority to tame anyone or anything. We humans, and especially our leaders, need to learn when, where, and how to tame ourselves. The metaphor of taming things is appropriate. Most of the world's large rivers, including the Mississippi, are tamed, or domesticated, in one way or another. Some, to our shame, have been used to the point where they are no longer recognizable as rivers. When that happens, people eventually just move away to seek their needs and wants—drinking water, quality of life—elsewhere. The fundamental challenges for society in this century are to realize the consequences of what's been done to nature in the past and to start reining in our wants. For centuries, rivers have provided immeasurable services to us, free of charge. Most of those services are still legitimate, vital, and possible, but they have never been infinite.

Quote the Old Guy
(with apologies to E. A. Poe)

Parts are failing.
Hair is thinner.
Tendon's wailing.
Back is sore.

Joints are creaking.
Eye-sight's iffy.
Cough and hacking,
phlegm galore.

Ears are hairy.
Knuckles swelling.
Ticker's scary.
Hearing's poor.

Passing gas is
entertainment.
Sends the children
out the door.

Getting madder.
Shrinking bladder.
Just a dribble,
never more.

Author's note: Miss Sophia lives along the Mississippi River near Dubuque, Iowa. She has watched the river and its people daily for sixty-four years. She is a recently retired high school history teacher. She fishes from her jon boat about twice each week, from April through October. She rarely ice fishes anymore. She spends some time each day in quiet contemplation. She keeps a journal.

A Preference
(from Miss Sophia's Journal, September 12, 2001)

There is nature. And there is man—a subset of nature. I prefer nature. She has a better sense of the ideal condition and seeks it much more faithfully.

The Ideal Condition

The River Is …

The river is my confessional.
The river is my hot tub.

The river is my Internet.
The river is my Louvre.

The river is my hero.
The river is my bully.

The river is my teacher.
The river is my test.

The river is my poison.
The river is my Prozac.

The River Is …

Dance Where the Big River Flows (a Waltz)

When I first met you, by the clear mountain stream,
you were still not much more than a girl.
I longed to kiss you. You were my dream.
But you smiled and turned in a whirl.

You said, "Patience's a virtue; there's plenty of time;
our love must be something that grows.
So let your heart travel, as I'll do with mine.
We'll measure how life's water flows."

The world wasn't pretty; every high had a low.
I had lovers, duties, told lies.
But seven years later, I remember it still,
what you said when I looked in your eyes.

You said, "Patience's a virtue—it's a silly old line—
but our love must be something that grows.
Our faith must be tested; our hearts beat in time.
So we can dance where the big river flows."

Then one day it hit me, how I was the one
that kept my love hidden below.
I've changed for good, as you knew I would,
and last night, you nodded—"I know."

You said, "Patience's a virtue, and our lives are bound.
Now I can see that it's true.
Our stream's now a river, we'll let the love flow,
and once more, our lives will be new."

So let's dance where the big river flows,
dance where the big river flows.
You'll be my partner, and our love will grow
as we dance where the big river flows.

Author's note: Anyone who has ever gone through boot camp has learned to march. After boot camp, I was assigned to the infantry and endured more weeks of training that required marching from one session to another. Someone would call cadence, often to the beat of a song. In jump school, we learned numerous versions, soft core and hard core, of the paratrooper song. I distinctly remember being so tired that one day I fell asleep while marching, but my feet kept going. Even now, after sixty-seven years, if I'm alone on a hike, I find myself silently counting cadence and singing to myself. I hope my lips don't move.

Reef Balls

I heard the other day that an innovative company that makes artificial reefs for fragile areas in the world's oceans also has a spin-off business: mixing cremated ashes into concrete "reef balls." The balls allow people who want to spend their next life with the fishes to do so, albeit with somewhat limited interactions. The balls are donated to government reef projects in an attempt to restore habitat diversity and substrates that will support diverse and productive food chains.

Sounds like a plan to me.

To be sung to the paratrooper tune "If I die in the old drop zone …"

When I die,
make no mistake.
Ball me up in
Lawrence Lake.

Bass and bluegills—
all will grin
as they nibble
on my skin.

Nutrients—
that's what I'll be,
doin' my bit
for eutrophy.

Spring Rising

(from Miss Sophia's Journal, March 1, 2010)

Winter will end soon here. It's over down south, but some river ice remains upstream.

If the Mississippi was truly an old man, what thoughts would be the first to enter his mind upon awakening this year? He might be surprised by how good he feels after such a mild winter. He might wince at new human plans for hydropower development or the memory of that benzene fiasco. And those Asian carp, like unwanted in-laws, are still multiplying, spreading out, and raiding the refrigerator.

Once again, he'd largely ignore the humans picking at his skin like birds on a musk ox. His attention would be on his sons and daughters, the tributary streams that supply his life's blood and bring excitement to the spring. He has been through a lot during his years: pollution, corn and beans, dams, levees. He's been able to weather these because the water has never stopped coming. To be sure, it's different now. It comes in unexpected spikes and at strange times of the year. But most of his creatures, plants and animals alike, know how to adjust to these changes. After all, they've been around longer than he has. Not many people realize that most river species came into being over twenty million years ago, compared to his short life of a half-million years. Humans, however, younger and still self-centered toddlers in many ways, haven't learned to live within their, or his, means.

He's been lucky. His job for over a century, moving boat traffic, hasn't changed much. His dams are not meant for water storage or flood protection like his brothers and sisters to the east and west. The Midwest still enjoys rain and snow aplenty, and his flows have not been permanently warped, although there is a lot more water in much of his floodplain. But no one has been so nearsighted, yet, as to think about diverting water from his valley.

He is getting old. He feels it more each spring. Those damn levees keep him from exercising. It's been a long time since he created an oxbow. He's putting on weight, sediment clogging his deep places. He misses the creatures he's lost as a result.

But rise he must. Already some of his creatures, the eagles, cranes, and walleyes, have started to stir. He doesn't value convenience like those lazy, two-legged pests. Though old, he still favors action. Usually slow, but faster in the spring, he'll soon be out exploring the nooks and crannies of his floodplain. Humans sit around at meetings and think too much.

Never Give Unsolicited Advice

The saying goes "Never give unsolicited advice. Those who don't need it will resent your arrogance. Those who do will think you're talking about someone else."

The heck with that.

1. Never complain about living on a shoestring to an elderly, barefoot lady.
2. When you need to cross unfamiliar ice, accept it quickly, and run very fast.
3. Think again before being content with low-hanging fruit. You may have to eat it.
4. Avoid the phrase "water level *fluc*tuations" during serious speeches to big audiences.
5. Check the plug before you back down the ramp.
6. If you have to pee on that electric fence to find out if it is on, perhaps you should consider trust-development training. Either way, you'll learn sooner or later. It only takes once.
7. Everything you think you know will eventually be proven to be conditional (or worse).
8. It isn't necessary to love the river. Just respect it, appreciate it, and give it the same care you give your garden.
9. If you don't have a garden, get one. You will learn the value of sunshine. It's not just for your tan.
10. Learn to be still. (Thank you, "Eagles" and all Buddhists!)
11. It's true—you can't dance to jazz.
12. Not only is life short; it's shorter than that.
13. Work hard, and you get to play hard. (Thanks, Dad!)
14. Very few people can offer more than a page's worth of good advice.

Author's note: The following poem is about relationships. For better or worse, I sometimes group my personal relationships into those with colleagues, those with family and friends, and those with strangers, people I know almost nothing about. Perhaps this is because it's become a habit of mine to communicate with each group differently. I, and perhaps many of us, rarely share our deepest feelings with lots of others. When we do, it can be clumsy and uncomfortable. My relationship to the river seems constant relative to my personal relationships. Some would say this seems a little disturbing. Could be. (Last, pardon my French.)

Upstream

The scientist—
well, he was pissed
and challenged my
objectivity.
Said, "You lie—
it defies
all the laws of gravity."

The woman didn't speak at all.
Her eyes flashed green,
but her shoulders slumped
as she understood.

The fisherman nodded,
continued to cast and reel,
cast and reel,
otherwise ignoring me.

Funny how people respond,
when I try to explain
how the river
has carried me
upstream.

The Visit

I was driving by and thought I'd stop to see how you're doing, Old Man.

Can't say you've changed much. Strong. Quiet. Still comfortable in that wet skin of yours. Still patient with me and my irregular visits, which I never seem able to predict.

You know, when we first met, I knew more about you than I knew about myself. Your reputation preceded you. How many words have been written about you, I wonder? How many are still to come?

It's hard to tell whether all the written attention has had any effect on you. I don't suppose it makes any difference. You'd still be you, one way or another. You always give more than you get. I like to think it was your persistence that helped me find my own path.

That path has meandered some, but I'm still here, too. Not rich, but still me—and content. My kids have grown into people I admire and respect, and that gives me hope for the future.

You'll be happy to know that they seem to respect you as much as I do. But that sets them apart from a lot of others. It's your future I worry about most. Many people these days don't seem to care about you or the future. Maybe they just don't see any of the connections that seem so obvious to us. Perhaps they don't feel capable or responsible for maintaining the connections, let alone making them stronger. That's why it feels so good to see you still doing your thing.

In any case, life goes on. I'm thankful for what I've got. Including your willingness to listen.

Still haven't been able to predict what I'm going to catch in some of your waters, though. The other day, I tried a new place, a remote side channel, pretty but shallow, and caught three huge redhorse. What were they doing there all by themselves? You usually send a half-dozen different species my way. No, I didn't think you'd be inclined to explain. We do have our separate ways of telling stories and keeping time. But every time I visit, it seems I relearn that there's more to you than meets the eye.

Okay. Less talk and more action. You can get back to what you were doing. I'll be heading home. I've got a couple of cords of firewood to cut and stack. Until next time.

Be well, Old Man.

Seeing the River

(from Miss Sophia's Journal, July 24, 2014)

Summer days, especially weekdays, tend to be quiet on the river. You can travel longer distances than usual, because of the slow current and calm air. The water-skiers are home or at work, Jet Skis in the garage. On these days, I like to throttle down the nine-horse and steer closer to shore to study shoreline details along stretches that I normally hurry by.

Over the years, my slow summer trips have placed me in the company of all manner of animals and birds. Kingfishers in particular seem to enjoy keeping pace with me, flying short distances ahead and waiting in an overhanging branch until you catch up. Late July is when the swallow parents are teaching their young how to feed on emerging mayflies, and beavers try to scare you away from their dens by slapping their tails on the water's surface. It's effective. A good tail-slap sounds like a gun shot. If you're caught by surprise, it can test your bladder control.

A couple of weeks ago, I saw a record number of turtles, thirty-five, on one long log that was just about perfectly laid out for their basking pleasure. That was right across the channel from the place where my neighbor's son, Ben, caught a four-pound smallmouth bass back in 1991. He was thirteen years old at the time. He had a smile on his face for weeks.

None of these things, of course, would interest my new neighbor, Louise, who says she will never visit the river, either on a boat or by foot. At some point in her childhood, she was apparently told by someone of importance that the river was dangerous and dirty, and she still holds to that belief. So many people seem to be happy to accept other people's beliefs and values, rather than spending a little time to check for themselves.

Louise would probably think I was starting to get a little daffy if I told her about what I saw yesterday.

Turtle Gathering

Warm and sunny, the day was also wonderfully dry. Occasional clouds provided just the right level of shade. We hadn't had any rain for a while, and the river water was clear. I pulled up to a sandbar for lunch. After a sandwich and apple, I took off my sneakers and carried a soda down to a spot where the beach gradually sloped out into the water.

I sat down on the sand with my feet in the water and let my eyes rest by looking into the water between my toes. The sun-heated water was just a little cooler than the air. In the shade provided by my hat, I saw movements. The skin on the water, carrying a gossamer layer of dust, was being blown upstream by the mild wind. Just below that, I could see thin needles of algae floating downstream. They looked like tiny grass clippings. I knew from a university seminar that this stuff is nicknamed "Annie-fanny" by the experts. Just above the sand bottom, hundreds of baby fish, each less than an inch long, swam upstream, about eight inches from the shore, as if on a highway, turning only when necessary to get around my feet. Through this tangle of minnow traffic, stray bits of waterlogged wood rolled downstream across the sand, at a speed of perhaps an inch every two or three seconds. My feet were acting like tollbooths on a multilevel turnpike of stuff moving both up- and downstream. A microdance that was captivating and easy on the eye, like watching city people and traffic from a sidewalk cafe. No collisions. Just small adjustments of things obeying complicated laws of physics and biology.

Such river mysteries are common. Happily, you don't have to understand them to appreciate the river's beauty, complexity or behavior. This holds whether you're looking at scenic vistas from the tops of bluffs or the water between your feet. You do, however, have to give your eyes and other senses the opportunity to perceive the parts and the whole. Can't do that by believing as Louise does. Her loss.

Author's note: Sara and I frequently listen to "A Prairie Home Companion." One January, listeners were invited to submit poems for the upcoming Valentine's Day show. Being a long-time fan of limericks, I sent in "Melting Ice and Snow." To our amazement, it was accepted. We bought tickets and sat in the audience as Garrison Keillor read it onstage, giving it the high praise of being a "good" limerick. The next day, I got an e-mail of congratulations from a cousin, Joan. I hadn't seen her in well over twenty years. Things that flow, indeed!

Melting Ice and Snow

Sara, I want you to know
your love melts the ice and the snow.
Mere words can't describe …
so I'll just inscribe—
X X O X X O X X O

Spring Break

Author's note: When I traveled for work, many of my trips consisted of the following venues: home airport, destination airport, hotel, conference rooms, destination airport, home airport. Personal travel is much more entertaining, and Sara and I travel well together. We like getting off the beaten path. I wonder if I could live like Travelin' Joe. What would it be like to walk the whole length of the Mississippi River?

Travelin' Joe

Travelin' Joe had a travelin' toe
that he followed, wherever it went.
He traveled north.
He traveled south.
He slept in a little pup tent.

Joe was a brown-eyed handsome man,
and the ladies all glanced his way.
He gave them honey.
They gave him money,
and they always asked him to stay.

But Travelin' Joe had a travelin' toe
that he followed, wherever it went.
He traveled east.
He traveled west.
He always made more than he spent.

Over beer and cards, I complained to him
that I never had a chance to go.
I loved my life,
and I loved my wife,
but some days I wished for that toe.

Joe said "Boys, we all got our joys,
and curses to balance them out.
On long, wet nights
I got no fire
or kids that laugh and shout."

Travelin' Joe had a travelin' toe
that he followed through rain and snow.
He traveled high.
He traveled low.
Where he is now, no one knows.

Mussel Rescue

Over the course of the last thirty years, the U. S. Army Corps of Engineers has gradually realized that one or two of the things it has done to the river may have actually had some negative consequences. Yes! It's true! Quite a change from the Corps' old demand that all of its projects be referred to as river "improvements," and one engineer's glowing opinion of his institution's role: "We control everything less than flood flows. Any water above that, we leave to God."

One byproduct of this enlightening has been an improvement in communications between engineers and conservationists, which has in turn resulted in changing, however slightly, the way the river's dams are operated. Biologists were able to convince the Corps that modifying summer water levels to mimic more natural river flows could be done without interfering with commercial navigation. Thus it happened that experimental drawdowns were initiated around the beginning of this century, and I had a much-needed attitude adjustment.

Drawdowns are simple. Normally, to keep the channel deep enough for barge traffic, summer water levels are raised by closing gates in a dam. One or two "control" points in the affected upstream "pool" serve as stations where the river's responses to the opening and shutting of gates are measured. Water elevation targets at these points have been established for each pool, and the Corps knows how to open and shut gates in both the upstream and downstream dams to meet those targets. A drawdown happens when the gates in the lower dam are opened slightly more than usual, dropping the elevation of the water in the lower part of the pool. In the summer, this provides young aquatic plants with more sunlight. When the gates are closed again, the dry period has made shorelines stronger for plant rooting. The plants grow and germinate more successfully, resulting in major benefits to other species that thrive in wetland and marsh habitats. Since the plants compete with algae for nutrients and filter sediment from the water, they also play a role in keeping broad areas of river less turbid—a recreational benefit.

But in 2000, nobody knew for sure whether drawdowns of only six to twelve inches (the limit set to maintain commercial navigation) would be beneficial enough to be worth the trouble. Under the heading of trouble, the Corps lists extra planning, science, public notices and meetings, and expensive dredging.

Experimental drawdowns were done to make sure the Corps and conservationists weren't forgetting something. One of those somethings was the potential exposure and mortality of animals that live on or in the river bottom where the water is shallow. Many of these critters, especially mussels, move slowly and are therefore at risk of being stranded. Most of the so-called experts (including myself) were of the opinion that mussels didn't occupy these areas in high numbers, and thus the risk was minimal. But the famous "mussel lady" from La Crosse, Wisconsin, Marian Havlik, argued otherwise.

We were wrong; Marian was right. A friend and colleague, Mike Davis (Minnesota Dept. of Natural Resources), joined me on the first day of an experimental drawdown to estimate the number of stranded mussels. We started at a marina near the anticipated upper end of the drawdown area. From there, we traveled to a handful of downstream sites, and it was clear that many mussels had been stranded.

Now, mussels can close their shells and withstand some desiccation for several days. That's part of their evolutionary adaptation for living in a system where water levels were historically unpredictable. But on this day, the mussels were getting a double whammy. Not only were they out of the water, but the sun was out in force. At noon, the temperature was well over ninety degrees. Even the mussels still in shallow water were suffering. By tracks left in the muddy sand, we could tell that some of the mussels were searching for deeper water by cruising over the surface of the river bottom. Others were trying to spiral down into the mud. Many were unsuccessful and were shedding pieces of gill tissue as a result of the heat stress. At one spot, the situation was so disturbing that we put our pencils down and simply started throwing as many mussels as possible back into deeper and cooler water.

Late that afternoon, after dropping Mike off at the marina, I drove home thinking about how hard it is to maintain adequate, let alone desirable, ecological conditions for all the animals and plants that call the river their home. As a scientist, my job was to provide accurate and objective information about the conditions that different river species prefer and require. But available information rarely goes beyond the most simple cause-and-effect relationships, and the river is one of the most complex ecosystems in existence. The frustration had been building inside me for a long time, made worse by the inability of most management agencies to work on sufficiently large project areas. Then there was the fact that many institutions don't resort to substantial action until something dramatic, perhaps even catastrophic, happens.

Seeing hundreds, perhaps thousands, of mussels dying that day was dramatic enough for me. I had a sandwich, grabbed a couple of beers and an empty five-gallon bucket, and went back to one of the worst sites we had seen. I arrived there about six in the evening.

The site, a sandy bar at the edge of a small side channel, was probably the remnant of an old natural bank that had once supported bottomland trees. After the navigation dams were built in the 1930s, wind, waves, and floods eroded away many of the new, higher elevation shorelines. The site was about fifty yards across in both directions, and its highest point was only about a foot higher than the surface of the river. The recently exposed river bottom, with its small waves of sand and mud, were crisscrossed from the tracks of mussels seeking water. There were a lot of mussels on the surface.

I ran the pontoons of my boat up onto a spot where the motor would sit in the channel. Then I got out and started picking up mussels and throwing them into deep water, hoping that they were still capable of righting themselves in the bottom and recovering from the stress. When I finished clearing the area within throwing distance of the shore, I started putting the mussels into the bucket and carrying them to the water's edge. I looked at my watch. I had a couple of hours left to clear as much of the site as possible.

My scientific habits kicked in during the tote-and-carry process. I counted each mussel, regardless of size or kind, during the first ten to twelve trips. It turns out you can get about thirty-five or forty mussels into a five-gallon bucket. I didn't have time to record the results on paper (doing so would have taken time away from the job), but I later guessed that I had picked up specimens of perhaps nine different species. This may seem like a lot to people unfamiliar with the river's mussel community. But the diversity was not unusual. It's not hard to collect between twenty and twenty-five mussel species in a day on the Upper Mississippi, depending on how many methods you use and which habitats you search. Records show that fifty-one species of mussels have been collected from the river, although several of those are now considered extinct.

When I was halfway to clearing the site, two fishermen in a small boated drifted by. After watching me make a couple of trips, one of them asked me what I was doing. I was breathing hard and could only muster a weak "Just tossing these mussels back into the channel." He thought about that for a minute and said, "Good for you!" and then returned to his fishing.

I checked my watch again. It looked like I was going to finish before dark. However, each trip put my next starting point a little farther from the shoreline. I needed to increase my speed, but walking that far across sand and mud with a bucket weighing more than twenty pounds started to make me acutely aware of long-forgotten leg and back muscles.

I finished clearing the site about fifteen minutes after the sun set. I threw the bucket onto the pontoon boat and myself into the river, where I stayed until my breathing returned to normal and most of my sweat was washed away.

On the way back to the marina, I drank my last beer and considered the consequences of my actions. I was well aware that the nine hundred or so mussels I had returned to the water were a small fraction of those that were at risk along the rest of the river. Furthermore, I could not be sure that even half of those that I'd "rescued" would survive. Even still, I slept that night with a profound sense of having done what I could, and my frustration about failing to make a difference was thankfully absent from work for a long time.

The experimental drawdown only lasted another day or two. Experts followed up with additional studies about the magnitude of the drawdown and determined that the procedure was indeed going to be a viable way to improve the aquatic plant life in the pool. A "real" drawdown was designed and implemented a year or two later. However, during the first days of that drawdown, which was scheduled to last several weeks, the river natural resource agencies gathered a fleet of boats together to transport about seventy-five volunteers—men, women, and children— to different locations to conduct the first, to my knowledge, full-fledged mussel rescue and accurately measure the drawdown's effect on mussel populations. Marian identified and counted the mussels, including some endangered species. I piloted one of the boats and had the great pleasure of seeing the faces of several kids who got to hold a mussel, right from the river, in their hands for the very first time.

Sorting River Mussels

Fur Brother's Rap

Lo! The muskrat—
small, demure.
Mussels are his
soup du jour.
Low-mound builder,
knows his mud;
builds again
after the flood.
Arrowhead,
surface "V";
midden mounds are
where he be.
Boom ka-chum, boom ka-chum, boom ka-chum, boom ka-chum.

Lo! The mink—
carnivore.
Handsome, sleek,
with incisor.
Fierce in combat;
ain't no dove.
Perfumed dandy,
suave in love.
Secretive,
stalking late,
along his border,
tempting fate.
Boom ka-chum, boom ka-chum, boom ka-chum, boom ka-chum.

Lo! The beaver—
lumberjack.
Lifting water;
tail whack.
Big Daddy-O,
of tooth and tail.
Trees are absent
from his trail.
Brothers, neighbors,
all for one.
Till humans
leave it
all undone.
Boom ka-chum, boom ka-chum, boom ka-chum, boom ka-chum.

Author's note: Scientists occasionally comment that data does not equal information. Too bad they stop there. Lots of people seem to think that there's not much difference between the forms of information. I beg to differ. A superficial attitude about the quality of what we know makes it hard for us to have constructive debates or to find common ground when the inevitable arguments do happen. Here's a tongue-in-cheek essay that describes some differences between some common terms. I tried to draw a diagram that shows the linkages between these terms, but the effort yielded nothing but a nasty headache. The linkages aren't linear. Still, it's a good idea, once in a while, to know something about the strength of the information you're using to make decisions.

Strolling between Data and Wisdom

> Where is the wisdom we have lost in knowledge? Where is the knowledge we have lost in information? —T. S. Eliot

Data

Data, being plural, are measures, pictures, tabulations, etc. By themselves, they are like a pile of logs not yet stacked or bricks waiting to be mortared together into a wall. The world is now chock-full of data. Would data exist if humans didn't think? Probably not. In any case, that's too deep for this discussion.

Observations

Observations can be based upon data or not. You can observe that one bird is blue and another is red, completely skipping any data. Animals, in addition to humans, have the ability to observe. Observations fuel curiosity.

Information

Information requires data or observations and allows comparisons. Someone observes that the leaves are falling and that the days are getting shorter. Or that today is warmer (colder, wetter, etc.) than yesterday. Huh! (One of my favorite scientific expressions). The Internet has lots of information. As my young daughter used to say when she was less than impressed—"Whoop de wow!" Information seems to be only rarely related to the truth.

Knowledge

Knowledge comes from making lots of observations. After I find my mail in the mailbox each day for three weeks in a row, I start to anticipate that it will be there tomorrow, unless it is Sunday. This helps me plan my day. It has value to me. Sometimes knowledge is associated with inductive or deductive reasoning, but neither of these is of interest to anyone but philosophers. Knowledge has its limits. You can "know" an awful lot about your cat or your kitchen. But does this knowledge help you avoid emptying the litterbox or make pancakes? A student who graduates with a degree occasionally has some knowledge, but not always. A drunk doesn't remember what he knows. He acts according to what he perceives (dubious observations) or believes (see below).

Experience
Experience requires knowledge gained repetitively and over time. A boater with experience knows that it's good to put the plug in before you launch the boat, *and* that it's good to take the plug out before a rainstorm when you're trailering the boat down the interstate. Experienced people know what will likely happen and won't happen under a wide variety of circumstances. Usually they're right; that's why they are called experts. They've spent time in many kitchens, making many meals, with different ovens and pots, and for different but usually hungry people. Experience allows a cook to know, given an electric range instead of a gas oven, how long it will take the range to reach a useful temperature, whether to use butter or oil, and what to cook in the first place. The experienced cook has the ability to predict that meat and potatoes satisfy most, but not all, people and that some consider a glass of wine and a chocolate dessert to be needs, not wants. This experience is admirable.

Wisdom
Wisdom comes when experts know when to use their experience and when not to. Sometimes it's just better to let things happen or let others lead, even if it means sacrificing something of importance.

Beliefs
Beliefs are the hardest to explain. They aren't necessarily dependent on any of the above items. Many beliefs are passed down from one generation to the next. Wise people have beliefs, but so do stupid people. Stupid people can be experienced, but they still aren't wise.

Some people believe in God and live a certain way as a result. My grandmother, who was Polish-Catholic and came over on the boat, barely spoke English. She believed in the Christian God. She was kind and loving but opinionated and judgmental. She was the matriarch of my mother's side of the family. There were times when I admired her more than any other person in the world. There was also the time I came home from college with a goatee and she said I looked like a Jew.

Scientists should accept that wisdom and beliefs are only randomly associated with each other. Too often, we expect science to influence people's beliefs. If influence is our goal, we need different trainers—perhaps people who sell vegetable choppers or pocket fishing poles. After all, if it's on TV or the Internet, true or not, it still motivates a lot of people.

Opinions

Opinions are cheap and easy beliefs. They have fewer standards than beliefs when it comes to describing the "truth." And as the saying goes, everybody has at least one.

Author's note: Haiku is attractive to me as a scientist. Like science, it requires the expression of a lot of thought using few words. A difference is that in science, ambiguity is frowned upon, but in Haiku, double or triple meanings are not only acceptable but desirable. Haiku novices like me tend to focus only on the number of syllables per line. Some written guides suggest trying to discover and perfect the turning point in each poem. I expect to learn everything about the style as soon as I understand quantum physics.

Haiku Trio

Gambling Strategies

> Humans nickel, dime.
> Rivers wait for big hands
> to play their wild card.

A Fool's Night

> Dreams of quiet wealth—
> honor, respect, peace—seem true
> until the sun rises.

Farsighted

> The old oak shades and
> offers gifts of firewood.
> Nurture the acorn.

Author's note: Although my memories are becoming a little suspicious these days, it seems that those from my year as an infantryman in Vietnam remain deep and razor-sharp. I easily remember expressions that were in common use then, and the title of this piece is one of those expressions. My rank was specialist fourth-class, equivalent to being a corporal in World War II. The conversations of enlisted men were mostly filled with slang and foul language. To be honest, there wasn't much good to say about our situation anyway, although I still haven't laughed as hard as I did on a couple of occasions when we returned to the base camp after three weeks in the jungle. We didn't have many behavioral standards, but the title of this piece reminds me that we were at least aware of our faults, still an admirable trait.

How Ya Gonna Act?

For your audience—go faster.
For your life—go slower.
For the world—lighten up.
For the job—hunker down.
For the family—be warm.
For yourself—be cool.
For the past—be forgiving.
For the future—be disciplined.
For today—be aware.

Off Days

As mesmerizing as the river can be, it is not a Sesame Street character, pleasant and warm 365 days a year. It can be overwhelmingly powerful and completely uncaring and indifferent. Some days inspirationally magnificent; some days like a gone-to-seed mistress—fat, smelly, and altogether nasty.

When we pay homage to the river, it's better to recognize all sides of its nature. Some people never learn. They get lulled into lack of attention, often even lack of respect. Then comes the lesson. Always catching them by surprise, the river ups and kicks them in the keister for behaving like spoiled, whining brats. They deserve nothing less.

Approaching Storm

Author's note: For well over one hundred years, the Mississippi River has been managed primarily as a commercial navigation channel. The driving force behind this river use is Midwestern agriculture. Barges carry grain downstream to international markets. The system of locks and dams on the upper river, built to create a nine-foot-deep barge channel, is heavily subsidized by taxpayer dollars. In 1986, Congress declared the river to be a nationally significant ecosystem as well as a nationally significant transportation system. Still, although parts of the river and its floodplain are managed as fish and wildlife refuges, laws prevent any restoration of river habitat from constraining the use of the river for commercial navigation. Balance between the two river uses continues to be a major challenge.

A River Fable

A friend of mine, crafty and old,
had no use for silver or gold.
But the river was captive
to men nonadaptive,
so here is the story he told.

There once was a river so great
it carried a million-ton weight
all the way to the sea,
to feed you and me.
One loved it for moving the freight.

The other one valued its fish.
Crappie was his favorite dish.
Two men and one stream—
a fat lawyer's dream.
Here's where the story turns piggish.

They started a hundred-year war,
each wanting his own special store.
Meanwhile the river
became just a sliver
of water that served them no more.

Its water turned smelly and gray.
Fools took the good water away
to serve other needs
and dubious deeds,
weird creatures now kings for the day.

One year, it drowned them in grief.
The next year, it fled like a thief.
They couldn't explain
the cause of their pain,
their ignorance beyond belief.

Neither man ever learned how
to look past the here and the now.
They placed no reliance
on sharing or science—
and died, for which death took a bow.

Will the river return now they're dead?
Its waters be our daily bread?
Our children will see
much farther than we.
Will they learn or repeat this instead?

Super Moon
(from Miss Sophia's Journal, September 28, 2015)

I haven't spent much time on the river at night this year. Fishing for flatheads—more specifically, lifting twenty-pound catfish into the boat—is starting to test my arm strength, and I'm already putting the pharmacist's kids through college buying pills to silence my bad knee. But yesterday, I put new gas in the tank and left the dock about six in the evening on a mission.

The weather guy on the local TV station had said there was going to be a once-in-twenty-year astronomical event starting at about seven thirty—a lunar eclipse. Not by itself so unusual, but this time it was going to be an eclipse of what they call a super moon.

The designation is a bit of hyperbole. The moon just appears bigger because it is closer these days to mother earth. But who am I to argue with anyone on TV. (Hah!)

I headed toward the east side of the floodplain and the Goose Island conservation area. I had a little camera with me and was hoping to get a nice shot of the moonrise over the Wisconsin bluffs and the numerous small side channels that flow among grassy islands dotted with silver maples and swamp white oaks.

Full moonrises near sunset occur about two or three times each year during the boating season, and I knew where the moon was likely to rise from previous fishing trips and a few youthful adventures, some with companions. After a pleasant, pulse-stimulating stroll down memory lane, I positioned the boat at a spot where I would get a nicely composed photo. There is a certain thrill to seeing the first little edge of the bright white ball as it creeps up over the darkening bluff.

Haze and smog, even on cloudless nights, often kills the rush. It's not uncommon to have to wait until the moon is a couple of finger-widths above the bluff top before its light starts to bleed through the dinge. But last night was different. The horizon was extraordinarily clear, and the few clouds left over from the warm, moist afternoon disappeared with the cooling temperatures as the sun set.

While waiting and checking the time, I remembered that the height of the bluffs along this part of the river delays sun- and moonrises by a few minutes past the published times. The times are apparently calculated assuming your land is flat (as if we have a lot of that in the Driftless Area[2]). Several pairs of egrets flew by on the way to their colony high in downstream cottonwoods. A flight of cranes, in traditional V formation, and lots of individual pelicans flew by in different directions, also likely toward their evening resting places.

My wait wasn't long. A little before eight at night, the top of the moon became visible, bright white, and knife-edged. I took three or four photos before it was fully exposed, hoping beyond hope that my arms, hands, and fingers were steady enough to get one sharp image.

It was then I remembered a promise to myself that I make on all nocturnal photo adventures—to reread the camera owner's manual about what settings to use to get the best pictures under limited light conditions. I had forgotten this step again. Well, if you aren't an expert, the only solution was to take *lots* of pictures. At this point, the camera was more of an expert than I was. I set it on automatic and started snapping but only for a few minutes.

Then I put the camera down and simply watched the moon do its slow, almost imperceptible walk across the sky. The trees on the floodplain began to throw moon shadows over the backwaters, which now sparkled in a light wind. Areas of submersed aquatic plants stood out, smoothing out the water surface. The dark silhouettes of a dozen pelicans passed just under the lower edge of the moon. That would have made a great picture, but there wasn't enough light. I didn't bother reaching for the camera.

Another twenty minutes passed without any evidence of the predicted eclipse. (I wouldn't see it, a startling view of the moon covered in an orange-gray stain, until a couple of hours later while walking the dogs back at the house.) I started the motor and began the slow trip back to the dock, having no trouble picking up the channel buoys in the moonlight.

I'll edit and cull the fifty or so photos I took down to about five or six over the next couple of days. No rush. It's just paperwork. The images are already safely secured in my mind.

Super Moon

The Saro Jane

I dreamed one night about a boat—
fair, and strong as bone.
A river queen on which to float,
content, to points unknown.

That morning as I walked along
our creaky village pier,
I saw her there. She'd drifted in
too quietly to hear.

I grabbed her line to
steady her and wondered whence she came.
A plaque upon her bow declared
she was the *Saro Jane*.

She rode up high and split the flow,
as easy as can be.
Who she served, I did not know.
I wondered, "Was she free?"

To emptiness did I request
to step upon her throne.
To my surprise, she whispered "Yes,
by all means—be at home."

I tied her off and came on board,
a thankful visitor.
Did she trust me? Hard to tell.
She seemed to not be sure.

The wind was gentle, warm, and dry.
It should've sheltered us.
But eerie rustles from within
bespoke a loneliness.

I asked if she would favor
a get-to-know-you ride.
"It's what I do," she answered.
"With that I can abide."

We cast off with a loaf and jug,
full moon to guide the way.
The stories that we shared that night
are with me still today.

We let the river take us,
not caring where or when.
Then back we came to home and rest
and did it all again.

At journey's end, when 'ere that be,
there'll be no tears or pain.
For I have had great fortune
and rode with *Saro Jane*.

Boat Trailer Blues

November's a time of drizzle and cold.
Again, I have waited too long
to take out the boat, dented and old,
a job for the stupid but strong.

The boat trailer lies like a sleeping black cur,
next to the garage in the mud.
Unwilling to rise, it gives me a sneer,
its brake lights the color of blood.

My gloves are too thin as I crank up the jack;
the burrs on the handle cut skin.
And now I'm aware of a pain in my back,
the vertebrae twisting like tin.

Three or four whacks with a hammer,
a handful of stinky brown grease,
a quick finger-jammer, a swear, and a stammer,
the hitch is connected with ease.

The half-empty tires are frosty, I see.
They suck at the mud as they turn.
In contrast, the bearings no longer turn free;
they slowly have started to burn.

Three colored wires atangle;
one light refuses to glow.
The other one shines, but at a right angle,
And now it has started to snow.

Exhausted and frozen, I am aware
that still I am only half done.
I hope that the next part is better than last year,
when down the boat ramp I did run.

This is the last time; never again.
I'd rather be home snug in bed.
To get all this pleasure out of November,
I'll visit my dentist instead.

Opposites

Rivers flow; engineers dam.
Oceans store; cities dump.
Trees provide; factories consume.
Weather varies; managers regulate.
Animals learn to survive in the world; humans learn to change it.

Nature draws squiggly lines; planners use a straight edge.
Nature dances to the seasons; soldiers never stop marching.
Nature likes itself; nothing satisfies humans.
Nature sings and listens; humans make noise and use earplugs.
Nature seeks harmony and balance; humans seek God.

Dance Again

Bury me? Oh, no.

The ground is too cold,
and those who reside there are too patient.

Give me back my youth,
when I rejoiced at every new breeze
and the warmth of the sun as it
overpowered the clouds.

Burn me. Burn me hot and fast.

Scatter my dust on the river—
the wet wind.

I'll watch the shore as she steers.
I'll rest in her backwaters.
I'll waltz in her eddies.
I will dance again.

Life and Death—and Life

Between 1979 and 1986, I ran a biological field station on the Illinois River, just upstream from its confluence with the Mississippi. My first wife, I, and our two kids lived about midway up the bluff in Grafton, Illinois. Many of the hollows that ran down into the main river valley in the area were too steep to develop. The creek beds were full of limestone cobbles and boulders. They contained so many geodes that Sara, my daughter, and I found enough of them to border a pretty big flower bed. The ridges and valleys were dominated by oak, locust, and honeysuckle. It was squirrel and deer heaven.

One day in mid-November, we woke up to one of those first hard frosts that sting your skin. For some reason, I had to get into work early. As the porch door swung shut, the purple-pink-yellow skyline on the horizon gave me pause. I heard my boots on the frost break the deep silence of the dawn. The brittle scratching of the plastic scraper against the windows of my truck seemed far out of place. I drove the three miles upriver to the station just before the sun rose, seeing no other vehicles on the road. As I stepped out to unlock the gate across the gravel path to the station, the white clouds of my breath drifted lazily back into my face. No wind. As I shivered, my fingers stuck momentarily to the lock. The silence was heightened by the cold. The chain clanked loudly against the gate.

I heard something crack far above and behind me and turned in its direction. More cracks followed. At first, I thought a boulder had broken loose from one of the limestone outcroppings. The commotion descended rapidly, and no more than a few seconds passed before the real cause of the disturbance revealed itself: A large buck broke through the brush where the steep gradient of the bluff leveled off. He was running at full speed and on a beeline, headed right for me.

My senses wasted no time jacking themselves up to full alert. But I did have time to think about what I was witnessing. Given the season, the buck was in rut, and he had picked up a scent. I wasn't an expert in deer behavior. In school, biologists quickly split off from general studies into specialty areas, and mine was aquatic biology. I knew a little about fish and mussels, but not much about deer. Still, being a young man myself, I was sure what his drive and focus reflected. He was ready—more than ready—for a good time.

That was the extent of my thinking for a while. I stood still and watched as he bore down on my position, snorting great clouds of steam, never losing speed. Thinking back on it, I was caught in one of those situations when the fascination of seeing, up close, a unique natural event prevented me from taking any action. The benefit is that you get to see more when you hold still.

For some reason, I never felt any threat or danger. Perhaps that was because, when he was about fifty feet from me, it became clear that he wasn't aiming directly at me. If he continued in a straight line, he would miss me by a couple of feet. Ever-vigilant, I remained frozen in place.

The moment of his passing is locked in my mind in slow motion. As he came to within ten feet of me, his gait changed. His front legs rose from the ground together and his back legs heaved. His head and neck stretched forward. Tucked, his front feet cleared the gate, which I had not opened yet, by a good two feet. The rest of his body followed in a graceful and perfectly efficient arc, with the exception of his tail, which stood at attention, straight and white. As he passed (within arm's reach), I looked him straight in the eye. If he registered my existence, it wasn't apparent. Then he was gone.

My mind started working again. The first thought that came to it was that he was using the station driveway as a path of least resistance. The second thought was a question: What will he do when he reaches the river? The station was about two hundred yards away; the river only twenty yards farther, on the opposite side. Would he pull up short or try to swim the quarter-mile to the other shore through very cold water? Vaguely reminding myself that I was the only witness to this event, I determined to see as much of it as I could. I swung the gate open, and my truck was rolling down the driveway before I even got the door closed.

Maneuvering the truck at speed gave me another minute to consider the rarity of the encounter. Somehow, even then, I knew I'd remember it for the rest of my life. I slid to a stop in the parking lot and ran around the building. The station was built on a creek delta. It was elevated about ten feet above the level of the river. The bank was protected by riprap, stone used to protect the bank form erosion. I could see easily across the river, as well as downstream in the direction of the rising sun.

When I got to the bank, the buck was already in the river, about twenty yards from shore. Deer are strong swimmers, although the shape of their legs seems to make for slow progress. The buck's V-shaped wake tracked a straight line that was directly perpendicular to the bank. His wake was the only mar on the glass-smooth surface of the water. It was light enough now for me to see details, and my vision was concentrated on the buck for a full minute or two.

Then something appeared downstream in my peripheral vision. A tow was coming upstream. There was no sound from its engines and no thumps from its bow as it slipped silently up against the seasonally slow, waveless current. People who boat on the river are familiar with such conditions. Tows can contain fifteen barges, three abreast and five in line. That puts the pusher boat far behind the front of the tow. Sometimes, while fishing, if you are facing away from an oncoming tow, its sudden presence over your shoulder can be more than just a little startling, making you jump immediately to the oars, anchor, or motor. This tow was made up of empty barges, as evidenced by how high they rode in the water. The lead edges of the three barges at the front of the tow were canted down and backward like the bow of any ordinary boat, to help the whole tow move smoothly through the water.

My thoughts about how silently the tow was moving were suddenly cut short by the realization that the tow and the deer were on a collision course. It was clear that even if he were aware of the deer (which he could not possibly be), the pilot could not change his course or speed in time to make a difference. The buck, a hundred yards upstream, was still unaware of the tow's presence.

Now my inability to do anything about the situation was more than just an inconsequential afterthought. The event I was hoping to mentally record so enthusiastically a couple of minutes ago had turned into a trap. I was going to witness something I very much did not want to see. A magnificent and powerful creature that had just shared an unforgettable moment with me was going to die in one of the worst possible ways.

When I think about what happens next, time slows down again. But it's not because my mind slows this part down. The slowness of the action in real time was agonizing.

As the buck got to a point about one-third of the way across the river, he became aware of the tow and that the distance between them was getting smaller. His path and progress had put him about midway across the front edge of the first barge on my side of the river. First, the buck seemed to slow down in confusion. Then, suddenly, he seemed to understand the situation he was in. His eyes expanded to the size of tennis balls. And, as the leading edge of the tow, which towered about ten feet above him, started to pass over his position, he panicked. As I watched, his legs started pumping furiously, but not to swim faster. He was trying to jump out of the water.

If you could freeze the moment in time, the image would have been odd but not alarming. It might have seemed as though the buck was taking refuge under the front of the tow. In real time, though, his behavior revealed the horror he was experiencing. In three more seconds, the tow was on him, slowly, silently, and unknowingly, as it continued its journey up river. The buck disappeared under the tow.

On shore, I was stunned. The scene, with the river of glass, the sunrise, the frost, the cold, was the same—and still beautiful. The world looked unchanged. Only I knew what had happened. As the tow passed, I thought, the first of many times, about whether there was a reason I was meant to witness what I had just seen. I am not a religious person. I don't believe in a God. But it didn't feel like I didn't believe in a God. Something seemed to be controlling the situation.

I continued to watch the tow. Perhaps twenty seconds later, along the side of the tow, near the joint between the first and second barges, a disturbance roiled the surface of the water. Something solid broke through. It was the buck's head. Rather than just bobbing randomly, he was moving back toward the shore. When he got about ten yards from the shore, he slowed. His legs found purchase on the river bottom. He walked slowly but steadily through the shallow water. He climbed out of the water near a large cottonwood that was yielding to the long-term process of bank erosion. When he was completely out of the water, he stopped, shook himself off, took a deep breath (again revealed by a small white cloud), and walked into the surrounding woods. I suspect he no longer remembered why he had tried to swim across the river in the first place. He didn't seem concerned.

That was the last I ever saw of him.

The river and the things living in and around it are amazingly resilient. Humans could learn a thing or two in this regard from our brother and sister species.

This Time, Next Time ...

Time is passing quickly now.
    Weeks can seem like days.

    The clock's last tick may still be far,
        but who can surely say?

            So these few thoughts are written
            to cheat the thief of time
            and carve my love for Sara
            on a tree of words and rhyme.

    Far better words than these of course
        have fallen by the way.

            Memories are frail things.
            Like twine, they wear and fray.

    But if there's life hereafter,
        and should that dream allow,

            I'll have the only path I need
            to carry out this vow.

    My love will find you o'er and o'er,
    no matter where or when.

        And to this tree
        I will return
        to carve
        these words
        again.

Lucky Again
(from Miss Sophia's Journal, April 2, 2012)

Five in the morning. Larry's Marina won't be open for another hour. But he has left the night crawlers I requested over the phone last night in a hidey-hole beside the ramp. "Preparation is all!" as Spenser, the fictional detective, noted regularly. There was a real man. His author, Robert Parker, passed away last year. What a loss.

My boot hits the dock, and the vibration travels over a hundred feet to disturb a sleeping great blue heron at the far end. He leaps with an ancient squawk, and heavy wing beats slowly pull him upward. He performs a backward indiscretion, and a trail of white splatters the surface of the water. I always chuckle when they do that, remembering my father, a WWII airplane mechanic, saying, "That gives them extra lift on the takeoff!"

At the boat, the checklist is short: gas, coffee, cinnamon roll, fishing rods, tackle box, life preserver, oars. The anchor rope needs to be replaced, but I'll be drift fishing with the current this morning and won't need it. Before I step down into the jon boat, I take a final land-based stretch and gaze over the point bar separating the bay from the river. The tree line on the far side of the channel is hidden in gray fog, but in two hours, warm sunshine will be at my back when I return.

No one else is in sight. It's the best way to appreciate the river—alone. Too bad the "back to nature" programs don't get this. It's as if people can't function as individuals anymore. But no point dwelling on the behavior of others. The motor turns over on the first pull of the cord. Lucky again.

There's a no-wake rule in effect to protect the docks and nearby boathouses, giving me a chance to sip some coffee on my way out of the bay. My rule is that the cinnamon roll has to wait until after the first fish is caught. It's more guidance than rule.

Before I reach the channel, I turn the motor off and let the boat drift. This is a good time for a short meditation. I'm not good at this. I envy the folks over at the Zen Buddhist monastery. They are the most peaceful people I've ever met. And they know you have to work at it. But I can't sit and just think about my breathing for longer than ten minutes at a time. I close my eyes and wait for the telltale increase in speed and the "tap-tap-tap" of current waves against the port side as the boat enters the main channel. The little outboard responds smoothly to the throttle, and I pull my cap down against the damp wind. Lucky again.

The Far Bank

I can see it there, in the bright afternoon sun.
The trees look familiar, like the ones I'm standing under.
That shoreline mirrors mine, the waves caressing both.
But it's there, and I'm here.
Stay or go?

Times change. This place is almost used up.
How much longer will it last?
The mud is slippery. My feet sink deeper and
turn blacker with each shift of my weight.
Stay or go?

Can't swim. The current is too fast.
Downstream is unknown.
Wading is my best chance—if it's not too deep
and the rocks don't break my ankles.
That too is unknown. Stay or go?

Only one decision to make.
No going back after the first step.
I know this place, not the other,
but it's not my choice after all.
Time to go.

Notes

1 Peter Coates, *A Story of Six Rivers: History Culture and Ecology* (London: Reaktion Books, Ltd., 2013).

2 At the junction of Minnesota, Wisconsin, Iowa and Illinois, the Upper Mississippi River drains a unique geological landscape called the Driftless Area. The area is exceptional because it was not scoured by recent glaciers, which left flat land surfaces and lots of gravel and boulders (drift) in their paths. From above, the Driftless Area, with its deep, forested valleys, looks wrinkled compared to surrounding agricultural lands.